Aleksandrs Čaks

Aleksandrs Čaks

Selected Poems

translated from Latvian by
Ieva Lešinska

Shearsman Books

First published in the United Kingdom in 2019 by
Shearsman Books
50 Westons Hill Drive
Emersons Green
BRISTOL
BS16 7DF

Shearsman Books Ltd Registered Office
30–31 St. James Place, Mangotsfield, Bristol BS16 9JB
(this address not for correspondence)

www.shearsman.com

ISBN 978-1-84861-674-5

ACKNOWLEDGEMENTS
Thanks are due to the Latvian Ministry of Culture which financed
the translation of this book, and the Latvian Writers' Union under
whose auspices the grant was awarded.

'Soul Fisher' and 'Night visitor' is reprinted from
Touched by Eternity, translated by Ieva Lešinska (Riga: Jumava, 2016),
by kind permission of the publishers.

Ministry of Culture
Republic of Latvia

Latvijas Rakstnieku savienība

Contents

Introduction   7

Joy   17
Ride in a Motor Car   18
The Song of the Sky   19
"Night"   20
Restlessness   21
Explanation   22
Crumbling Time   23
"Tonight I chased my heart"   24
Placards   25
The Last Tram   26
Bermondtian Officer   27
Young Lady with a Dog   28
A Life   29
Maria Street   31
Sailor in Patent Leather Shoes   32
To the Neighbourhood Lamp   33
Romance   34
Chopin's Funeral March   35
Three Books   37
On the New Pontoon Bridge   40
On the Narrow-Gauge Railway   41
"In the barn"   42
"Oh the greatest horror...."   44
"In an evening"   45
Song for the Cabbie   47
Spring in the City   48
City Boy   49
Answer   50
Lyrical Poem   52
Invitation   53
Two Variations   56

Elegy in a Window   63
What Did he Mean by That?   65
A City Night   67
Self-Portrait   68
Ice Cream   72
It's Bad   73
Tonight   74
Rifleman's Song   75
A Latvian Girl Sings to a Rifleman   76
For You   79
Drainpipe   80
Train   81
Ballad of My Joy   83
Nature   88
Where I Will Sit Tonight   90
I Yearn for Another Form   91
The Ring   93
Mirror of Fancy   95
My Roach Ensemble   97
Restlessness   101
Letter to a Dead Newspaper Woman   105
Soul Fisher   109
Night Visitor   112
Speck of Dust   120

Introduction

Aleksandrs Čaks (1901-1950) is one of the most popular and best-loved Latvian poets of all time. Even though his life was relatively short, spanning less than 49 years, his literary output was substantial, including poetry, short stories, and criticism. His verse has been set to music on numerous occasions, including two melancholy favourites, 'Confession' and 'For You', which most Latvians discover by the time they reach adolescence, and learn by heart so as to be able to join in singing them at the Midsummer Night's bonfire. Čaks's striking appearance, his bald pate, and round glasses, make him instantly recognisable even to people who have never read his poetry. There is a monument to Čaks in a Riga park, and a street and a literary award named after him.

Čaks's life was full of the various contradictions and mysteries typical of his fellow Latvians, a people that had experienced two violent revolutions – in 1905 and in 1917 – to which was then added the First World War, the Latvian War of Independence, the Russian Civil War (in Čaks's case), sixteen years of Latvian democracy and four years of Latvian dictatorship, followed by Russian and German occupations, and then another Russian occupation, this time in its cruel Stalinist phase. These situations required the talent of a tightrope walker, balancing one's aspirations against what was allowed, second-guessing the often murderous powers of the State, while trying to preserve one's dignity *and* survive (two often-mutually-exclusive goals).

The future poet was born in Riga, the only child in the family of a successful tailor with the official name Jānis Čadarainis-Čaks. The son later opted to keep only the shorter part of the surname. The family's relatively comfortable middle-class life in Riga, a culturally developed, diverse European city, which had become one of the most important industrial centres and ports of what was then the Russian Empire, was disrupted by the First World War. Along with hundreds of thousands of other Latvians, Čaks obeyed Russian propaganda and the direct orders of its military that quite literally called for a scorched-earth policy. The plentiful harvest of 1915 was burned, along with the farms that had produced it in the Latvian countryside. The machinery in Riga's factories was either evacuated or destroyed, and the whole of Latvia was emptied of its people. Latvia's population never returned to its pre-First-World-War size.

With the high school where he had commenced his studies, Aleksandrs was evacuated first to Võru, Estonia, and then, as the Eastern front drew nearer, to Saransk in Russia. During this time, he read widely in philosophy, but was particularly interested in the works of Kant, Nietzsche, Fichte, Hegel, Schopenhauer, Spencer, and Bergson – for the most part in Russian translation. Having entered the Faculty of Medicine at the University of Moscow in 1918, for the next year or so he participated in student literary events organized by young Imaginists and Futurists whose ideas proved to have a lasting influence on him.

There is no information on what Čaks thought of the revolution of 1917 – Saransk was rather remote from its epicentre in St Petersburg and, at only sixteen, he was too young to participate in any meaningful way. Yet, by all accounts, it was in 1917 that he wrote his first poem – in Russian – the poem's bombastic title, 'O Rise, Ye Holy Latvia', seems to indicate that he had not lost his connection to the land of his birth. Nonetheless, there is no doubt that Čaks was swept up in the revolution and its aftermath. In 1920, when a peace treaty normalised relations between the nascent Soviet Union and Latvia (which had proclaimed its independence in 1918), many Latvian refugees, Čaks's parents among them, returned to their devastated native land. Čaks, however, remained in Russia. Early that year, he was drafted into the Red Army as a paramedic and sent to work in various army hospitals and on a sanitary train. Documents uncovered in the Yeltsin years, when the Russian archives were relatively open, indicate that, in this period, Čaks (then still Čadarainis) repeatedly appealed to Russian authorities to allow him to move back to Latvia, yet every time his request was denied. Then, curiously – but perhaps as a logical consequence – Čaks decided in November 1920 to join the ranks of the Russian Communist Party. As a result, his serious career as a Communist apparatchik was launched: he was appointed head of the propaganda section of the Saransk region's Communist Party Committee and spent the next couple of years travelling the area establishing party schools and showing himself as a true believer in the Communist cause.

Why are all these details important? Because a couple of years later, Čaks received the coveted permission from Moscow to return to Latvia – apparently in exchange for the promise that he would bring important documents to the small Latvian Communist Party, which, from 1920 to 1940 operated underground, and to act as liaison between it and the Soviet Communists. Whether or not Čaks ever kept any such promise is, and will probably remain, unknown. According to his contemporaries, the documents in question remained in Čaks's possession even through the German occupation during the Second World War and he made no special effort to conceal them. While there is still no clear explanation for these mysteries, when speaking of his years in Russia, he referred to them as very "dark, heavy, and filled with mad adventures and feelings".

However, nothing in Čaks's life and work in independent Latvia suggested anything sinister. Having come back in 1922, the *anno mirabilis* of *Ulysses* and 'The Waste Land' in English literature, he fitted right in with a generation of young poets and artists traumatised by the war and its aftermath, and eager to transform that trauma into works of art that represented a radical break with the past. Yet for Čaks and his contemporaries, theirs was not the relatively settled existence of Eliot or Joyce. Čaks's friend, the poet Pēteris Ķikuts wrote:

> The world war and the subsequent revolutions are over. [Our] wounds are healing. The face of this century is scarred by bullets and shell splinters. Splotches of drying blood ... desperate faces ... pain ... and suffering ... And next to all that: a passionate desire to live [...]. It's not just towns and villages that have been devastated, it's not just [...] meadows and [...] fields that have been gashed by trenches: the human psyche has also been devastated and gashed. [...] Having come home, the Man of the World takes off his grey great coat, takes off his boots caked with blood and mud, washes his hands and face, looks at himself, winces and suddenly becomes aware of a horrifying question: "Who am I?" [...][1]

What modified this stark existential mood was the fact that, in contrast to young poets in Western Europe, Čaks and his peers faced life in a newly-born country, a canvas from which much of the old paint was diligently being scrubbed and which offered an opportunity and a platform for a whole new, vibrant picture to emerge. In 1925 – when Čaks had recently published his first poems in a Latvian press, and he was still a teacher and school administrator in the Drabeši municipality of northern Latvia – the society of artists, Zaļā vārna [Green Crow], was established by young painters interested in breaking away from the traditions and conventions of pre-war Impressionism and Neo-Romanticism and willing to wade boldly into the latest modernist currents rushing in from the West: Expressionism, Cubism, Constructivism etc. Among the

---

[1] *Latvju modernās dzejas antoloģija*, Riga: Grāmatu Draugs, 1930, p. 7

additional interests of Zaļā vārna was the bringing together of people involved with varied creative pursuits. For this reason, Čaks, along with other literati, found a natural kinship with the visual artists, eventually joining the editorial board of the society's magazine and persistently – and successfully – urging that the group establish a publishing venture in addition to its other activities. Despite a chronic lack of funds, Zaļā vārna managed to publish a number of books, among them Čaks's third and fourth books of poems: *Pasaules krogs* (World Tavern) and *Apašs frakā* (Guttersnipe in Tails, 1929). His earlier chapbooks, *Sirds uz trotuāra* (Heart on Pavement, containing seventeen poems) and *Es un šis laiks* (Me and This Time, with thirteen), published in 1928, had been the publications that brought him to the attention of Riga's intellectual and artistic circles.

It is not difficult to see why Čaks took Riga by storm. No one had read poetry like this before in Latvian. The broken line, the accented metre, the free verse, not to mention the striking similes, metaphors, and other non-traditional means of poetic expression – all this was new. So was the protagonist, the 'I' voice in the poems: it was a street urchin or a young man, alternately full of bravado or anger against social injustice, irreverent and at times slightly world-weary. Because of this, and the oft-mentioned drunkards holding forth in bars and dives in Čaks's poetry, some readers tended to confuse the poet with his poems. His critics were already outraged by poems that had appeared in periodicals. Was he that modern youth who would say to women: "I want you, / you see. / Drowsy talk / always / of theatre / soul, / art / let's leave them aside. / Give me your lips, / let me untie your ribbons – / enough, / time is money"? Interestingly, he was attacked both by the left, in the person of the writer Linards Laicens, who called Čaks "reactionary", and by the right, represented by Rihards Rudzītis, who criticised his "ideology of hooliganism", "bar psychology", and "pessimism".[2] Yet his fellow writers spoke of a "serious, diligent, and active man; shy, kind, very polite, and always well-groomed". Modern psychology would probably find that Čaks's rowdy 'ultra' bohemians and cynical adventurers compensated for some part of his soul. Adventurousness and negligence were totally alien to Čaks's nature. For a little while he made an attempt at pretending to be full of mystery and fatalism, dropping a jarring remark here and there and gulping down drinks, even preparing at one point to throw

---

[2] Richards Rudzītis, 'Negatīvas tendences mūsu visjaunākajā dzejā' (Negative Trends in Our Latest Poetry), *Daugava*, 1929, 9.

something of an orgy, but soon he gave up with a smile, recognising that he could not fool anyone for very long. With time, he even became so well behaved and modest that friends took to calling him Papa Čaks. "I have never seen this extoller of drunkards and tramps drunk, angry, slovenly, unshaven or in any other way defiant of bourgeois convention."[3] As for women, they have left reports of a gallant gentleman who would bring them flowers and handwritten copies of his poems and cook for them. Women loved Čaks, even though the typhoid fever that he survived at an early age had not only made him lose his hair but seemed also to have affected his virility. As for Čaks himself, he answered his critics by stating that he and others were trying "to pester current society by showing how deplorable it is. With their pessimism, the young poets would like to make modern man open his eyes, so that he can see clearly the stagnant puddle of quotidian life in which he is cosily sitting".[4]

Bohemian or no, in poetry Čaks felt kinship with such free, adventurous spirits as François Villon and Lord Byron, yet his main influences were those of the Russian modernists: Blok, Mayakovsky, and Pasternak, as well as Akhmatova and Yesenin. A keen observer of people and the very fabric of ordinary people's lives, his leftist views made him a natural fit with another literary magazine, *Trauksme* (Alert), which published from 1928 to 1931. *Trauksme's* editors believed in the social function of poetry, its ability to expose society's underbelly, and eventually help in bringing about a more just and equitable arrangement, with spiritual values paramount. They turned their backs on lyric poetry inspired by the bucolic Latvian countryside and its religious ideals, which combined Baltic pantheism with Lutheran piety, welcoming the city with its factories, ports, slums, dirt, and social problems. Čaks seems to have avoided the most radical leftist positions espoused by *Trauksme* – he officially joined the Social Democratic Party, which had split from the Bolsheviks in 1918, and remained a member until the right-wing coup in May 1934 – but, in his poetry, he always sides with the underprivileged and the marginalised – the street-urchin, the street-sweeper, the street-walker, the street vendor. The world he loves to depict is the *nomales* of Riga – incidentally, one of the words that presents a problem for the translator. Usually it is translated as 'suburbs' or 'outskirts', yet I am quite certain that neither word would evoke for the English reader

[3] Anšlavs Eglītis, 'Atmiņas par Aleksandru Čaku' (My Memories of Aleksandrs Čaks), in *Mana mīlestība* (My Love) New York, NY: Grāmatu Draugs, 1958.

[4] Aleksandrs Čaks, 'Kādēļ mēs esam huligāni un pesimisti' (Why We Are Hooligans and Pessimists), Daugava, 1929, 10.

the visuals that are immediately available for the Latvian one. *Nomales*, the outlying districts of Riga, were borderline spaces between the modern city and the countryside that existed even as late as the 1960s when I was a child. Aggressively claimed by the industrialisation of Riga in the 19th century, these areas were built up with blocks upon blocks of dwellings for factory workers, most of them first-generation Rigans. Often, the flats were dark, cramped and lacked basic amenities, such as running water. To compensate, former farm women often developed beautiful gardens in the courtyards, growing not only flowers but also fruit trees and vegetables. It was not uncommon to keep chickens, a goat or even a cow in the shed to provide one's children with fresh eggs and milk. The quiet *nomales,* with green foliage overhead, sandy side-streets underfoot, and wood-smoke wafting into one's nostrils, possessed a special charm as a kind of liminal space between the old, rural Latvia, and the new, modernising one.

In that outlying world, there was an establishment which also had a regular presence in Čaks's poetry and for which, again, there is no suitable word in English. The Latvian word, *krogs,*[5] comes, etymologically, from the Swedish word *krug*. During Swedish rule in 17th century Livonia, a *krogs* – a place for travellers to rest and feed their horses, an inn – was supposed to be erected every two miles. As Latvia became a part of the Russian Empire in the second half of the 18th century, the *krogs* gradually lost its function, turning into a place where alcohol was sold and consumed. To this day, the word is used in conversational Latvian to refer both to a dive and to a high-end bar, but the associations with *krogs* in Čaks's œuvre are more poetic and existential. For Shakespeare, the world may be a stage, but for Čaks, it is a *krogs*. In his long, dramatic poems, *Poēma par ormani* (*Poem on the Cabbie*, 1930), *Spēlē, spēlmani* (*Player, Play*, 1944) and, especially, *Matīss, kausu bajārs* (*Matīss, Prince of Drunkards*, 1943, whose subtitle reads 'Poetic Drama or a Merry Play with Four Corpses'), he makes them more than plain: *krogs* is the time-space where we encounter one another, where our subconscious is given free rein, where "we all are drunks and sots / swilling life as best we can".

Čaks's poetry collection *Mana Paradīze* (My Paradise, 1932), with its thoughtful structure,[6] its development of themes found in the boulevards of the modern city, its *nomales* and its mastery of poetic technique, meant that he could no longer be dismissed as a mere hooligan, forever at odds

---

[5] In this book, I have translated it as a 'bar' or a 'dive', depending on the immediate context. In other contexts, it might also be translated as 'tavern'.

[6] Čaks also included the best poems from his previous, shorter collections.

with conservative society. The last poem in the book is titled 'Lieluma ābolā kodējs' – literally, 'One Who Bites into the Apple of Greatness' – in which his poetic persona admits to his ennui, but by which he no longer wishes to be distracted; he is encountering a new and poignant urge to break free and take a bite out of the "apple of greatness". This 'apple' for Čaks turned out to be his work on a set of long poems dedicated to the Latvian Riflemen who defended their homeland against the Germans in the First World War and then fought in the Russian Civil War and Latvia's War of Independence, showing legendary bravery, yet tragically, often serving interests other than their own. The first volume of this cycle, containing eight poems, was published in 1937, with the second, containing fourteen poems, appearing in late 1939 after the Molotov-Ribbentrop Pact had been signed and independent Latvia's days were numbered, and Čaks, himself, had only a little over ten years to live. The subsequent occupations – Soviet (1940-41), Nazi (1941-1945), and Soviet again (1945-1991) – prevented Čaks from carrying out his plan for two more parts of the 'Heroic Epic', as the whole was later subtitled. While intended as a paean to the heroism of the riflemen and, by extension, to the Latvian nation, the best parts of *Mūžības skartie* (Touched by Eternity) lack the excessive level of testosterone and pathos present in some of the verses – one of Čaks's strong suits is his attention to detail, the particular, the individual, the intimate: soldiers shaving and putting on white shirts before battle; the colour of battleground mud; the air that is "split into shards" by machine-gun fire. The feeling of being right in the middle of it all is enhanced by Čaks's use of body-parts as metaphors: "a black mouth that can clamp shut, silence holds them between its teeth", "Nervous like an eyelid, air quivers; / The big shelter is trembling like a lip", etc. His most moving lines are reserved for the same street urchins and guttersnipes from Riga's *nomales,* so lovingly described in Čaks's early poetry and now the protagonists in a historic drama.

The fact that Čaks wrote most of *Touched by Eternity* during the period of Ulmanis's authoritarian rule found its reflection in his poetry in that he downplayed the role of the riflemen in their support for the Bolshevik coup and their fight against the enemies of the new regime, which was in part inspired by Lenin's hasty peace deal with Germany and promise of independence for Latvia. While official criticism frowned upon the leftist world-view espoused in some of the poems, the authoritarian regime approved of their overall positivism and rewarded Čaks with praise and prizes. When the Soviets occupied Latvia in 1940, Čaks, in turn, was

13

reprimanded for right-leaning tendencies in the same opus, yet he was permitted to become a member of the official Writers' Union in 1941. With the German occupation, Čaks was banned from publishing but did write a few poems, publishing them under the name of his last love, the translator Milda Grīnfelde (1909-2000), to whom he dedicated his book of poems *Debesu dāvana* (Gift from Heaven, 1943).

The second Soviet occupation, following the Second World War, proved fatal for Čaks both as a poet and as a mortal human being. Fearful of the Soviet regime – one that had murdered many of his erst-while literary colleagues who had ended up in Russia after the First World War, or after escaping the dictatorship of the late 1930s – a regime which might take umbrage over his success in "bourgeois Latvia", he produced poems about the repaired water supply, the rebuilding of factories, the stakhanovite movement, not forgetting to sing to 'You, My Moscow' and the 'Father of the Nations', Joseph Stalin: "Our happiness will rise with the sun: / To vote for Stalin will be our fun" and even more embarrassing lines that almost suggested mockery – not so much of the grotesque regime as of his own poetic mettle. Yet the regime pounced on him. In 1947 he was dismissed from his work at a newspaper and from then on his poems – both the postwar poems and the ones from the 1920s and 1930s, were closely scrutinised, practically word by word. As the literary historian Rolfs Ekmanis has observed: "Three chief reasons were given for Čaks's heresies: his unsatisfactory knowledge of Marxism-Leninism, his decision to spend the war years in German-occupied Latvia [instead of evacuating with the Soviets], and his reluctance to join the Marxist underground during Latvia's independence."[7] Čaks, who had written about the world as *krogs*, now took to drinking excessively in real bars. Milda Grīnfelde recalled how, after receiving another of the regular doses of harsh criticism about the 'bourgeois nationalism' evident in his poems, Čaks wallowed drunk in the snow in one of the parks where he used to stroll, well-groomed and dressed to the nines, and she could not get him up. Čaks died of heart failure in Grīnfelde's apartment, having not quite reached the age of 49. Grīnfelde, his 'gift from heaven', was a year later deported to Siberia for translating French literature and discussing it with friends and was only able to return to Latvia in 1956.

What is Čaks to Latvians? One of his 'disciples', the poet Ojārs Vācietis (1933-1983), summed it up in a 106-line poem 'Čaks', from

---

[7] Rolfs Ekmanis, *Latvian Literature Under the Soviets: 1940-1975*; Belmont, MA: Nordland Publishing Company, 1978.

which I will quote just a few lines:

> …He died without leaving behind
> Any commandments
> Carved with insensitive hands
> In the heart's cold concrete.
> He left behind him
> Eyes full of wonder,
> Romantics
> And hooligans,
> Himself at times being as frail
> As a hair wrought from glass,
> Himself full of doubt and maturing
> Like the bud on a giant tree.
>
> But when in Riga's Old Town
> There comes and ineffable evening
> Reminiscent of Čaks,
> Which no words, no kisses, no songs can exhaust,
>
> People's thoughts
> Delve down to the well of his verse
> And come up with a luminous bittersweet world,
> All of it. […]

Ieva Lešinska
September, 2019

Joy

Joy stirs up our blood
       like a cow wading through a spring.
It's like moist breath on a mirror, joy on our clarity.
Joy is part of an animal, joy is a burp.
Only an aeroplane, telescope, lift and – pain
Raise us up like prayers.

1924

Ride in a Motor Car

Past the Air Bridge, the car leaps like a tiger, flashes like a boomerang.

It swallows miles like sweet berries, the swish of the tyres a friendly greeting.

The passing telephone poles and trees begin to look like fingers pressed tightly together.

We flash by like a falling star past gangs of boys and women who bear gossip instead of children.

The wind remains, this sadist and born thief – it steals thoughts, robs us of breath and pulls everything off our heads,

And the speed becomes a passionate man, he takes me, he possesses me, my heart goes numb like a foot.

So much open space in my heart, so much excitement, every rocking motion of the car mixes my hair with the blue of the sky,
offers stars to my lips and moon's breath for my cheeks.

Past the bridge, past the bridge, the auto leaps like a tiger, flashes like a boomerang.

I salute you, you lacquered dolphin!
I wish my heart would beat at your speed.

1925

The Song of the Sky

Why are our eyes so pale blue? Why is our hair like straw in mid-August?

Because we like to look at the sun and the clouds. We love the wind, wind alone and hate the earth, we love the air that quivers above the earth, and the stars that evening brings us from outer space.

Because we do not love the earth, which we leave, opening our souls like eyes, like chalices toward the greatness of sky.

We hate the earth, bringing ourselves royally over it like a foot over a puddle, so that everything that the earth bestows upon us, passion, suffering, love, and hate, would run off us like water off a round ball.

We only love the wind, the playful wind that makes our hair so pale.

1925

[Night]

Night.
I stand by the open window.
Monotonously the clock behind me counts the stars.
The moon hangs on the horizon like a monstrous drop of blood.
Fog creeps secretly through the bog to the hill like a platoon to a battle.
Silence stares from all corners and listens, agape, at my heartbeat.

1925

Restlessness

Again the day, another day is over,
Just a few footsteps echoing in the street.
I sit alone at my table, sober,
My heart beats, yet desires peace.

It's burdened by a weight or strain
That always, always stings and stings.
It's that small fever – restless pain,
Which stirs up all that seems to wane.

Like a morning wind that churns the lake
It stirs my mind's lucidness
And wages war without a break,
And brings about my spitefulness.

1925

Explanation

I am a scream of an era drowning in a sea of blood.
All these words, which pile up in my verses as if
        drunk – they are splinters of teeth
        knocked out of my gums by desire.
They have been seasoned like meat with my curses
        and tears, which I have shed in pain and in hunger
        and swallowed down instead of bread.
If you tore open my chest, you would not find a heart
        there: a grenade has been thrown and
        keeps exploding there, destroying the last vestige of
        peace and lucidity, tearing off taps like buttons
        from the pipes of bile and unrest.

1925

Crumbling Time

Like old brick walls our time is crumbling,
Spider's webs are sparkling in the sun,
And yet it turns its toothless mouth
Toward all of those that smile in the sunlight.

Like old brick walls our time is crumbling,
Yet as it falls it wants to bury
All those who feel like grinning
As it evaporates like a morning mist.

Like old brick walls our time is crumbling,
And yet it's ready to set to and fight
With all of those who hate and curse it,
Before the new era rises radiant and bright.

Mid-1920s

[Tonight I chased my heart...]

Tonight I chased my heart out on the street
To go earn bread, for hunger's nearby.
I don't have a santīms for a bath
And desperation burns like a distant flame.
I am tangled up in life as in debt and feeling
My days pass by in thought and in pain.

Why guard clarity and fragile moments?
No, not such nonsense is not for our time,
Youth breaks everything like spare oars,
It lives impatiently, but without coming into bloom.
Roaring speed has arrived with aeroplanes,
We laugh and seek our peace from bullets.

I chased out my heart. Do I expect it back?
Sweet oppressive void where my heart once was,
Sweet tiredness has turned my feet to stone
And I can never be free of it.
And where could I look for my former heart
With this face distorted in pain?

1927

Placards

Placards, placards – city's soul –
colourful, garish like ladies' stockings,
blood red, yellow, and black,
they accost me from corners, gates and posts,
more insistent than harlots at night.

Placards, placards, city's sacraments,
schedules for plays, bars, and meetings,
I love you, love you as much
as in my boyhood I loved
football, boxing, and ice cream waffles.
Your motley essence,
your contrasts, your broken lines
are so close to my heart.

Placards, placards, best prescriptions
for my impatient soul.

Sirds uz trotuāra / Heart on Pavement (1928)

The Last Tram

The last tram to Riga
leaves the stop
without ringing its bell.
On the last tram to Riga.
Three women sit,
I sit opposite
and in the corner
sits a drunken man.

The last tram goes faster than usual –
wobbling, shaking and growling.
The conductor is out on the platform,
swaying with the rhythm of the tram and his nap,
he doesn't hear
the man growl along with the tram
a song about the rosy-cheeked youth
whose leg was taken by the battlefield
whose bride was swallowed by the voracious street;
he doesn't hear
the women's sharp voices about prices
rising ominously
like curses,
like unrest among people,
but I feel
these conversations pierce me
like shards,
like stubble pricking a bare foot,
and I feel my flesh and my thoughts sweat out
the rosy intoxication
I had received
from a girl's lips
under an apple-tree in the orchard.

Sirds uz trotuāra / *Heart on Pavement* (1928)

Bermondtian Officer

Yesterday
in a dive
I suddenly
ran into
a Bermondtian officer.

Flustered
and sharp
as if after a slap
I
jumped to my feet.

In my
clenched fist
the glass crumbled
like a bud.

With a smirk,
he got up,
with a smirk,
he finished his glass
and
vanished through the door.

I didn't say
a word to him
that night,
not a word.

I kept my words
like so many bullets
for another,
a worse occasion.

Pasaules krogs / *World Tavern* (1928)

Young Lady with a Dog

In an Old Town side street, narrow
like the slit of a post-box,
where noise and bustle merely echo
where it smells of tar, iron, and apples in dry cellars,

I met a young lady –
handsome and agile
like tongue,
like a violin's bow.

Her shoes were patent leather, black,
with red stripes and green heels.
Her face, an amandine oval,
was lit up red
under her hat, a huge glowing coal,
and her lips
seemed to be oozing blood.

She rushed
like seltzer from an uncorked bottle,
like water down a slanted gutter
and nervously tugged along
a dog on a brown leather leash –
as big
as a blacksmith's fist
and legs wobbly
like jelly.

She rushed
with steps that cascaded
like apples from an upturned basket,
for a thunderstorm was approaching
billowing over the tiled roofs
like smoke from a large chimney
pierced by flames here and there.

Sirds uz trotuāra / Heart on Pavement (1928)

A Life

On Gertrud Street
by the Mishkinsky furniture factory,
smarting with pain,
I overtook
a middle-aged man,
some petty bureaucrat
or shop assistant,
for it was already past seven
and sun was gilding the windowsills.
His face
was serious
and almost grim,
like that of a cashier counting out millions,
like that of a surgeon, beginning to cut.
And he walked
slowly
with a pound of sugar and herring,
for it was already close to four weeks
since his wife had died:
his wife –
sweet as the sun,
with hair
the colour of autumn leaves –
golden;
his flat was
disorderly,
empty,
with the kitchen door open,
for it was almost four weeks
since he had walked
slowly,
as if exhausted,
and he carried,
steadying with his hand,
a little boy on his right shoulder,
carried him

like Jesus of Nazareth
carried his cross
to Golgotha.

Sirds uz trotuāra / *Heart on Pavement* (1928)

Maria Street

O, Maria Street,
monopolised by
Jews
and night moths, –
let me
sing of you
in verses long and sleek
as the necks of giraffes.

Maria Street,
you tireless trader,
sun or moon,
you buy and sell
everything
from junk
to divine human flesh.

Your vibrant body
tells me
what that speckled snakeskin,
my soul,
shares of the century with you;
it's so restless,
it's so nervous,
so dashing and darting
like a panting dog's tongue.

O, Maria Street!

Sirds uz trotuāra / Heart on Pavement (1928)

Sailor in Patent Leather Shoes

On the boulevard double-breasted with lamps
and nicely coiffed lindens,
I met a sailor
in shoes of patent leather, two shiny spears,
and with a chest that swelled like a mainsail.

His face was the brown
of a copper coin,
of a polished oak wardrobe,
and he moved like a restless wave.

He must be a magnificent lover –
a character
like seltzer,
like powder,
with no harbour for rest.

His eyes were the colour
of cat's eyes,
the green of leaves and rust
mixed with sky-blue.

His eyes were cat's eyes
in colour
and shameless like women
and dogs in the month of April.

He had just come ashore from his ship,
hungry for love more than for bread,
he carried ashore from his ship
the smells of tar, herring and sea
brought to Riga from Ghent.

He had just come ashore from his ship,
patent leather shoes on his feet,
he was a pool overflowing
and hungry for female flesh.

To the Neighbourhood Lamp

You yellow lamp, why stand there on the corner,
Day and night like a permanent guard
In this grim neighbourhood with so many mourners
With faces so grave, sad, and hard?

Cover your light, be sure to be slow,
Burning out like a dying man's stare,
So that the faces darkened by shadows
Don't see their own horror in your radiant glare.

For their suffering and for their pain
You are but a reflection, superficial, unneeded;
Your place should be with the vain
On the streets rich and with emptiness seeded.

So that they can avoid the fright
That smirks at them all day from the start,
They need a strange and beautiful light
Light that flows like love from the heart.

Sirds uz trotuāra / *Heart on Pavement* (1928)

Romance

I live amongst the downtown walls
where my garden is
a flowerpot placed on a stool
and a handful of last summer's heather.

There are no rivers wider than gutters,
no lakes deeper than puddles,
where, warmed by the sun,
children splash from basement flats.

Nature is revealed
in orange peels
dropped on pavement
and radish greens in the rubbish bin.

Instead of nightingales at night,
I hear shingles squeaking in wind
and cats meowing on the rooftops.

And yet I love it all,
as much as my betrothed,
I love the city centre
with its broken streets.

There,
my window wide open,
I can stare at lamps instead of starlight
and get lost in reverie
about the people
who built it all
so I would need it quite as much
as I need a pulse,
as sails need wind,
as a ship needs steersman and screw.

Sirds uz trotuāra / Heart on Pavement (1928)

Chopin's Funeral March in a Dive

In a neighbourhood dive,
dirty and black
like its customers,
I sat with my friends
and drank.

At the next table
sat some Poles
singing in unison
about the slavery of yore,
of war,
and the burning eyes of their women.

A full-bearded Russian
whispered in my ear
about his son,
a commissar in Russia,
and about his own suffering
in Wrangel's army.

A drunken locksmith
punched his wife
because
she wanted to go to their children.

Suddenly,
a worker
with blackened face
stood up from his table,
threw a coin to the musicians
and ordered:
"Chopin's Funeral March!"

"Outrageous!"
my friend jumped to his feet:
"Chopin's Funeral March" – in a bar?

A waltz,
a foxtrot –
any time:
let the tinkling motif
glow under the fiery violin bows
like coals under breath!

I left my hand in the Carpathians –
you think
it was just a greeting to Austrian ladies?

My last strength
seeded the Tīrelis peat-bogs
yet now
not even a crooked pine grows there!

I need joy,
not sorrow,
joy that stings,
that's fierce
like pain,
like a girl's tears after her first pleasure,
joy!

Chopin's Funeral March in a bar?!
As if the one ordering
were not a worker
but an undertaker
who has entered
calmly
with a coffin
to take us all
like dead bodies to the grave...

"Yes," the worker replied,
and the mournful motif
began floating
over the bowed drunken heads.

Pasaules krogs / World Tavern (1928)

Three Books

I published a book,
nice,
on eternity,
    art,
            and the soul.
I published it,
but all the shops
one by one
sharply
declined
to stock my book.

Was I sad?
No!
I published a second
book,
a passionate book
on brotherhood
  help,
            the future of mankind,
                    and its noble culture.

Yet one looked
in vain for it
in the shop windows
amongst novels in beautiful bindings
modern inkwells,
and lean cinema beauties –
in vain.

And when,
having entered the shop,
I asked for a book,
my passionate book,
a young lady, aromatic
as a classy cigar

and with a gentle Madonna's face
smiled:
"This is no shelter
or animal aid society."

And then
on this foggy autumn evening
when under the boulevard lindens
instead of flowers
there was only the scent
of street girls
and cars emerged from the dark
with two burning suns in the front,
I
returned home,
pulled off my boots, throwing them out the window,
I sold my coat to the landlady
to secure my room,
then I sat down
and
wrote a book:
Practical advice for
            treasury pilferers,
            promissory note counterfeiters,
            murderers,
            singles,
            would-be writers,
            those failing graduation exams,
            chauffeurs, and
            clumsy dancers.
Twelve big publishing houses
fought for it
as if it were state funding.

And when this book came out,
thousands
of dazzling
neon advertisements
transmitted
the title of my book.

Next to
famous Dunlop tyres,
Chlorodont toothpaste,
and wonderful Hubigan powders,
from all corners,
posts and showcases,
my face
faced yours –
narrow and gaunt,
after sleepless nights
and dinners consumed only in dreams.

The shouters
hired by the company
called out:
Viva!

Tramps and schoolboys wondered
as they looked at my portrait:
"Is this some yogi
or a self-starving record-breaker,
perhaps a Japanese boxer,
or a murderer on the run?"

Young ladies sighed:
"O saviour of our souls!"

And
a modern
tobacco factory
produced
its best cigars
with my name on them and
using its worst tobacco.

Pasaules krogs / World Tavern (1928)

On the New Pontoon Bridge

On the new Pontoon Bridge
where snow
whirls around me, insistent
as old laws, girls, and churches
on every corner
with their upturned boastful noses;
where a boat wheezes on the Daugava
blinking
its sole lamp by the chimney
like a passerby's cigarette
its smoke growing
like a frost-covered tree in the dark.

On the new Pontoon Bridge
I met a gentleman.
He possessed as much portliness
as a pork roast on a white dressed table,
and my soul,
which I had lowered deep down,
squirted
pitch dark hatred and anger –

so that I'd use my fist
and put out like a lantern
the calm in the fleshy face
reclining in it
like a sparkling gem
in a fancy setting.

Sirds uz trotuāra / Heart on Pavement (1928)

On the Narrow-Gauge Railway

Night.
Station.
Lights like yellow rags.
The conductor whistled for the tenth time,
but the train wouldn't move.
The conductor whistled for the eleventh time –
same result.

Sitting in a car small as a restaurant sandwich,
I
struck a match for the tenth time
but it went out.
Sitting in the car,
I
struck a match for the eleventh time –
same result.

And then I pulled open the window,
to let in fresh air,
and then I pulled open the window
to wake up the train driver.

The train whistled and began moving.
Fresh air streamed in,
and the match glimmered red
like my heart.

Sirds uz trotuāra / Heart on Pavement (1928)

[In the barn]

In the barn
that used to
house horses
noisy pictures are shown.
Chaplin laughs
on the chalky screen.
And young
working women
with lacquered fingers
like Easter eggs
and powder masks
shake with excitement.
Fleas
shiny brown
like resin
crawl
up a leg
like the Eiffel Tower.
And rats, old and grey
as if frosted over
leap over feet.
Their tails
are long and tough
like ropes
on which one can hang oneself.
In the streets,
where sand
used to steam
dry, soft and yellow
like porridge
Swedish stones are
lined up and listening.
But
working class girls
are enraptured and sad,
they are

already lacquered.
The pungent and sticky odour
of horses
remains in the
walls and ceilings,
mingling
with the scent of powder
and people's breath –
nightingales' open beaks
swallow the world
drop by drop.

Late 1920s

[Oh, the greatest horror...]

Oh, the greatest horror of this era is that –
that factory smokestacks
buildings and aeroplanes
can already climb higher than the human heart.
And the World War?
The War measured up against this
the way a spittle is against the one spitting.
Man, for you to find your own heart,
do you need a 100-watt bulb?
And even then
where heart should be
there will be only rush
like the one on railway platforms,
cool,
and gluttony greater than that of a bank.
Oh, the greatest horror of this era is that –
that factory smokestacks,
buildings and aeroplanes
can already climb higher than the human heart.

[On an evening]

On an evening,
a windy October evening,
a drunken man
stood under lindens in the dark
and passed into the gutter
the beer he had drunk.

That evening,
motor cars
passed him by
turning off their lights.

Lonely damsels,
upon seeing him,
threw up their collars.

Falling leaves
rushed down the street
rustling like silk.

The high
lonely lightbulbs
that strollers
tended to confuse with stars.

At a meeting
a famous professor
held forth on eternity.

At the opera
the fourth act
of *La Bohème* just finished.

Mary Johnson and Dita Parlo
kissed nobly on screens.

At a fine bar
six hundred perfumed pairs
started to tango.

A woman
on Dzirnavu Street
gave herself away
at a 30% discount.

At a neighbourhood dive
someone cut open another's head
with a broken bottle.

On the next street
at the foundry
a worker
lost an arm.

And the radio announced:
it's been found, it's been found –
a radical means
against pregnancy.
Yankees in the State of New York
no longer favour marriage
and mutiny number sixty-four
is underway in Mexico.

On an evening,
an October evening,
a drunken man
stood in the dark under lindens
and passed into the gutter
the beer he had drunk.

Late 1920s

46

Song for the Cabbie

My dear cabbie,
you street-corner Don Quixote,
in your velvety cart I feel
like a baby
in an ancient pram.

You
rock me
gently like old verses
and nice stories
about Old Town streets.

The clatter
of your horse's shoes
seems like bells
from a forgotten church
that everyone passes by.

My dear cabbie,
you are
the sadness of all that once was,
the last greeting of the city
to barns and outlying fields.

You took me
to the graveyard
or a painful farewell
where mourning wafts
like the scent of a beautiful woman.

And riding with you
I feel like writing
a poem
on the back of your coat,
a prediction of your demise.

1929

Spring in the City

The gutters are fragrant again,
and their dirty tide runs chocolate brown.
The pavement has thrown off its snowy fur
and welcomes human feet.

The yards are cleared of snow. Sewers steam,
And there, insubordinate and free,
The wind gathers up wonderful aromas
And sprays them on the street.

No time for cinema. The sun shines all day long,
Park benches wait for you.
On a wall, I even saw some flies today,
And cockroaches too.

And in far-off neighbourhoods
where your boots get filled with real mud,
Boys still play their coin games
For feathers, keys, old tsarist roubles.

Apašs frakā / Guttersnipe in Tails (1929)

City Boy

O, former pig herders, listen to me –
I'll come to your aid, a city boy
Soaked in the smells and curses of the streets,
Hating all that is peaceful and staid.

I am still as I was in my boyhood,
Crazy, spittle in my mouth, like a dog:
I had no one to teach me what's good
Unlike you with your lambs and your hogs.

That's why you like to make your pipe sing,
To dream and mourn under the willows,
Whereas I like to whistle and swing,
And push life along like a cartload.

My dad has worked as a sweep and a cop,
I will not cuddle you like a boa.
I've let my heart drop into the gutter,
And so what if I'm disliked?

I learned from spires and chimneys
Even before dying to enter the sky,
And streetlights have taught me
To spite the dark and not let the light die.

Let's not stand around like carters,
Freezing and waiting for a cue
Drinking with me would be smarter,
You dear former pig herders.

Apašs frakā / *Guttersnipe in Tails* (1929)

Answer

The wise ones say I should write
about things
        that have more of the eternal;
my poetry, they say,
reeks of the carnal,
and has too many
        drunks,
                thieves,
                        and street urchins,
girls
who, barely sixteen,
accost the first passerby.

Messieurs and comrades,
if it makes you ashamed,
then
        simply
                blind me
as Bermondt's gang
did to some Latvians,
or
get rid of all
        drunks,
                cabbies,
                      and thieves,
exterminate them
with that green Japanese powder
they use for bedbugs,
turn
streetwalkers
        and tramps
into ladies and gentlemen,
nail shut the basements,
raze the outskirts,
take women's
hearts

and plant them in rows –
and yourselves?
Don't enter any dives
that –
     I believe you –
          irk you so much,
don't secretly chase
after women
on autumn nights
and make them
undress
for a mere eight lats.
But
while
I see it all
day and night,
while
I
keep falling into it
like a cesspool
to drown,
I will scream –
and I
can't and mustn't
not scream –
for
I find it repulsive
to talk sweetly
about your toadying
yellow souls,
those rotten teeth:
I
  am no lackey.

1930

Lyrical Poem

It was early spring.
Cars
bestowed mud
        brown
                as coffee
                        as varnish
                                as Cuban cigars
on ladies
free of charge.

I
looked in the window
on a dozen kinds
of tropical fruit
and dreamt of Spain,
of women, ardent, impetuous
like film stars,
for ladies passed me
        freezing like cellar steps,
dressed in precious furs
that cost as much
as I would need for a year
to visit girls and write verses
on happiness.

1930

Invitation

My friend,
don't sit in the evening
on the stairs,
don't look at the stars:
they are like poets –
brilliant only when dead.

Look,
in the basement flat
street-sweepers light candles
and are sitting down for supper
rattling their spoons
in cheap dishes
with the sound of a tram.

Damp,
paper tin,
weary fog settles
on pavements.

Moon is
the yellow of butter.
Too bad,
I have no
knife or bread
and
no one to go and fetch them.
A yellow dream sandwich
would come in handy
right now.
And quietly
we would sit together.

I would rest my head
on the floating clouds
that are your knees.

And I would feel
your fingers
on my fevered head –
the cool drops of rain.

Look –
the fog has reached the moon,
gossamer
like a fly's wing.

Trees are afraid of darkness,
they shiver with sweat
cold
like a brass handle in winter.

My friend,
don't sit
on the stairs.

With thirteen pieces of wood
I will light the fireplace
in my room.

I will take the pillows
from my bed,
put them on the floor,
and cover them
with a blanket
from a Kirghiz tent.

In vain
night will try to press through the window.
I will draw the curtains,
the softness and thickness
of hair.

Quickly
I will take off
your shoes
and put them under the bed.

We will sit
by the fire
so close
that our clothes
will begin to steam
like horses in lather.

The bird of silence
will land
on your lips.

You
will sit
in my eyes
as if on a lap.

And
I will tell you the story
of the boy
who walked from yard to yard
and showed people tricks.

Mana paradize / My Paradise (1931)

Two Variations

1.

Riga.

Night.

The yellow omelettes of streetlights lay in puddles.
The rain
rattled cherries in suburban orchards,
drumming on leaves,
throwing pits in the canal.

The sky
was dark like a window
covered in black cloth.

What could I do
on a night
that required galoshes?

Shave my soul's beard?
Play on my nerves like a piano?
Swallow dreams like oysters?

What could I do?

So I went
to a bar on Moscow Street
where thieves and streetwalkers gather
to grieve.

Osram bulbs
swayed slowly above my head
like yellow amber earrings.

Ice cream
the colour of orange
melted on my crystal plate
in a small puddle
like a cut eye.

Somewhere
a zither breathed a bacchanal.

The night
wrapped the round bar
in the black and crisp silk of the dark.

The nearest linden
dropped a leaf
on my lonely table.

I picked it up
and kissed,
for I had no lips to kiss.

Lips?

Why should I
kiss any lips?

Why can't I
kiss the marble top
of the table
as clean and cool as a girl's mouth,
or the wall,
this same wall
that supports
a woman's flesh,
plump and white like melted lard?

Oh, why is it that a girl's lips
possess the monopoly to cure
the ache of a mouth!

Perhaps
so that I'd sit here
alone
with endless desire
writing strange verse
about myself
one who loves
a girl's lips more than anything else.

2.

Riga.

Night.

The clock struck
twelve.

The orange carnations of light
suddenly wilted.
Darkness
over the puddles
like black, gleaming silk.

How was I to wait for the morning?

Eat plums,
tear at remembered scabs,
beat the rhythm
of tango
with my finger on teeth
and drink sadness by the glass?

How was I to wait for the morning?

And I went
to a seedy bar
where there is no parquet

and thieves and streetwalkers come
to grieve.

I
sat in the corner alone
calm and gaunt as a monk.

Beer
in a mug
bloomed in front of me
yellow orange
but my lips
were thin and dry
like birch bark.

Why was
I sitting here?

Why?

Outside time flew
like a bird
when girls welcome
sucking kisses
and hands
that help them untie their shoes,
open the side buttons
remove the stockings
and like shed snakeskins
toss them in the corner.

Why was
I sitting here?

Had my mother died,
had a friend
left me like a broken ski?

What were you hiding?

Hiding?
Yes!

Why
can't you
scream like a siren
to tell everyone
of your smarting, burning pain
and desires?

Get up
and tell them
how alien and repugnant
you find these couples
gliding past
and swaying in painful thirst
as if wanting to dance naked,
tell them
that this red light
is stabbing into your eyes
like a sharp spear –
tell them!

What?
You are silent?
Afraid?

Or do you think
that words in this room
are redundant,
in this room
soaked in red light,
music wails
and women talk
no – blab
their passion to men's desire
with their hips,
with shiny bared knees
and still covered breasts,
you think?

Nonsense!

You
sit here
calm and gaunt as a monk,
yet watching
if waiters might be shrugging
if waitresses might be grinning
and streetwalkers –
if they
might be shaking their heads:
"Poor poet,
he must be ill
or wounded somewhere bad."

You fool,
do you want to become their laughingstock?

Get up and bang,
bang your fist on the table
so that
the beer mug
flips over
like a shot rabbit
and the flower vase
becomes airborne
and ends up in the floor's clutches
to be broken in pieces,
bang your fist
and say:

"You,
you who think
that I'm weak,
you, who are only a moment,
the grey film of dust,
a wounded fruit
that will rot before its time,
you,

if I
don't secretly peek
under every girl's blouse,
if I
don't rush
to some corner phone booth
after every
kiss that's like warmed on a primus
then – you – think,
you fools
that I don't know love?
No,
I even pray to the idol of passion
and I love;
I love
and will go on loving,
but in my love
        I yearn for eternity.

Mana paradize / My Paradise (1931)

Elegy in a Window

The moon tonight
       seems to be pickled.

For a family
on the fourth floor,
the gramophone plays.

From the street
twilight and chill
flow in.

I feel
like a sailor at the port of Bergen
looking at the ice
       through his binoculars.

Nevertheless I dream
I'm in Paris
where I could kiss in the street.

You are a midinette,
I'm a mediocre poet;
we sit in a smoke-filled room
and drink the cheapest
of French wines.

You smile
       at my fantasy scene.

It's the time
when the last of the Sunday people
return home from the seaside.

Streetlights
come on above the lindens
lining the squares.

But we
don't even have lindens;
just an old myrtle
and memories of pine needles
in the vase on the table.
And I'm as sad
as a neighbourhood girl
who's lost her favourite cat.

Mana paradize / *My Paradise* (1931)

What Did He Mean by That?

It was a sweltering hot day.

A cripple, a ragged, disabled veteran, had fallen on the stairs
    where rich people lived.

Was he simply exhausted? No, it was a quick and definite death:
    his face was white as a screen and his breath remained
    still in his lungs.

He had fallen hard on his back. By his navel, where the
    trousers ended, perversely gaunt and bluish brown flesh
    was on display. His mouth was open to the blue sky like
    a well, like an extinguished crater that had vomited
    nothing but curses and longing for happiness.

His arms were crossed on his chest like torn, slack ropes, and flies
    ran like salesmen on his dirty and stinking hands. Were
    they looking for coins he might have reaped before death?

A crowd had gathered around shaking their heads, perplexed.
    Someone mentioned an ambulance. – Phew, – a woman
    countered: – He should be taken to the morgue and be
    cut open. He must be infectious.

– What drivel – someone muttered annoyed – we have caught
    the infection of need already. Then he went up to the
    body and leaned down to look at the fading features.

– I know this man – he then announced – He fought against
    Bermondt's gangs. And then he's been staying at our
    night shelter. I'm the janitor.

And having separated the crowd like a thicket of shrubs, he went
    off to look for help and take the dead man to the morgue.
    A group of boys walked off with him, looking at him
    with respect, admiring how well his hat sat on his head,
    how long were the strides he took.

And the dead body? – It continued to lie there. Only his shrivelled, crippled legs, cut off at the knees and covered with leathery caps he had raised up at the crowd and windows of rich people like threatening gun barrels. What ever did he mean by that?

Mana paradize / *My Paradise* (1931)

A City Night

Outside my window
no scent of mignonettes
or lindens full of bees –
thrown in a pile in the yard
as firewood
are old car tyres and some shards.

Like a flower
opening its petals,
the rubbish bin yields scents
awaiting rats,
centipedes,
and a stray dog's presence.

Pebbles on the ground
radiate the gentle warmth
of a primus that's cooling:
this strange
and vibrant silence
is like a quiet ruling.

It's broken by the watchman
loudly sighing,
keys jingling
when he has to open.
And rare is the car that passes,
a red carnation in the back
and in front, two tea roses shining golden.

Mana paradīze / My Paradise (1931)

Confession

Window weeps in the mist. I have to admit:
I have loved no one but you.
Is it wine that moistens your lips
So they glow as if drenched in red dew?

Where the boulevard steams, I met you once,
I have known no rest ever since.
On that corner where a tramp begs so coarse
Desire will trample me like a horse.

I wander the streets day and night,
Plucking leaves in hopes that I'd sight
Your kiss or a strand of your hair,
Then I drop them empty and bare.

I gaze into windows as I walk by
Maybe I'll see the shine of your eyes;
But this hope is but the flight of a bird,
The tick of moments is all that I've heard.

Where are you, my friend? In that glow
That a lone cloud has bestowed?
Or are you this desire that breaks
Through my sharp verses' ache?

Window weeps in the mist. I have to admit:
I have loved no one but you.
It must be my blood that moistens your lips
So they glow as if drenched in red dew?

Mana paradize / My Paradise (1931)

Self-Portrait

Midnight like chloroform
closed people's eyes.

Pocket watches
set out in the dark on tables
counted the breaths.

I
wandered the boulevards alone,
I wandered and wandered
as if trying to count the stars
with my steps

Melancholy passer-by,
have you seen a man
stooped in an alley
sitting
next to a trampled banana peel
and a paper scrap –
sitting,
palms to the ground?

Have you met a man
who rejects the cinema flyers
kindly distributed on the boulevard
and catches a yellow leaf
floating down to the ground?

Have you noticed a man
who, cheek pressed
to a grey five-story wall,
is shattering the nearby lamps in his mind,
so as to watch, like a somnambulist
the shiny corpses
of dead stars?

Melancholy passer-by,
that man is
I.

There was a time
when stairs and the infested lift
taught me
to strive upward,
but stairs and lifts
are content with the seventh floor –
not I!

Builders,
carpenters,
why don't you build
houses with a hundred and ten storeys,
towers
on which clouds could
perch like birds
and the moon at midnight
partake
of a traveller's meal?

On the space
on the roof
where the breath of vanished souls
and the scent of clouds
can be felt,
pressed up to a chimney,
I
would hold forth about love.

And then I would see quite well:
clouds
are like scented powder
that a smiling lady
dabs on her nose.

And then I would understand quite well:
even the moon
whose mysterious light
allows the exchange of sweet kisses
with trembling girls
in the alleys
is made of yellow saffron
that cannot be touched.

And then I would feel quite well
that just like a distant cloud
and the moon,
in thirty years
I will be only a vanishing breath
a dissolving handful of dust
that will not even cover
a bush in the alley…

Midnight like chloroform
closed people's eyes.

Pocket watches
set out in the dark on tables
counted the breaths.
I
wandered alone through the boulevards,
I wandered and wandered
as if trying to count the stars
with my steps.

Mana paradīze / My Paradise (1931)

Ice Cream

Ice cream, ice cream!

How many times have I
ridden the tram without a ticket
just so I can have you!

Ice cream,
your waffles
bloom for money
on all city corners,
those waffles
golden and beautiful
like tea roses in boulevard shops,
your waffles
reddish like blood
like women's lips and the night-lights of cars.

Ice cream,
for you
I have sold my best coins,
my rarest stamps
with tigers multi-coloured like shop windows
and giraffes tall and sleek like radio towers.

Ice cream,
I have felt
your etherlike cool
keener
than a girl's lips and even my fear,
you,
calendar of the age of my soul,
loving you
I learned to love
all longing and life.

Mana paradīze / My Paradise (1931)

It's Bad

It's bad –
I am a Latvian poet –
of what shall I sing?
My heart
is dry and thin
like the neglected leather
of an armchair.

If I were a Negro poet,
I would sing
of lips
dark and warm
like nights in July
without stars or wind,
I would sing
of girls' flesh
brown and firm like the earth,
I would sing songs
of freedom so distant
as clouds in the sky –
if I were a Negro poet.

But now?
To us now
freedom is bad,
girls are too skinny,
they paint their lips like canvas,
we have radio towers
and rubber soles
for walking –

quiet like cats,
we feel quietly,
think quietly,
and die quietly, too.

Mana paradīze / My Paradise (1931)

Tonight

Tonight I want to dream
of everything taller than spires.

Sitting in the square
on the bench where a tram rambles by,
do you feel scents wafting from meadows,
fragile and gentle like rain?
Birches stand there
       reaching toward the blue sky
themselves white as if in nightshirts.
Mock-orange scent wafts.
Cows sigh in their barns.
I could dive into hay,
the kissing hay
in lofts skimpy as wages.

Tonight I want to dream
only dream
and forget the need for money,
the holes in my shoes
and that tomorrow
      I must find work.

Mana paradīze / My Paradise (1931)

Rifleman's Song to a Latvian Girl

If you are sad, my friend,
don't,
just don't go to the circular café on the hill:
there are only ladies
who smell of the best lipstick,
Eastern perfume,
and their lovers' cigars,
there is a Jewish violinist all too handsome
and some youths
who spend hours over a single cup of coffee
secretly watching lonely young women.
…Don't go there.

If you are sad, my friend,
come to me.

I have a burnt down candle
in an empty black balsam bottle,
a small brown card table,
which I bought yesterday,
and a glass of sailors' vodka.
Come.
I will spread my coat on the floor,
the moon will shine at us through the window
and doves will coo softly on the neighbouring rooftop,
and I will sing you songs
about birds and water.

Come…

Mana paradīze / My Paradise (1931)

A Latvian Girl Sings to a Rifleman

Let's go
to your room in the outskirts
where the corridor smells of live chickens.

There, until dawn,
we'll sit on the floor
close together
on your old greatcoat
that bears bloodstains, dark red and solid like lacquer.

I will wear a yellow silk headscarf.
A shiny cockroach will scurry across the floor.
Dying,
a fly will buzz quietly, entangled in a spider's web
and in the garden outside, fruit will grow like dough.

Night,
blue like the water of lakes
will press on the window,
that window
whose cracks you cover with wax
when it's cold.

To make it darker,
we will cover the bulb
lightly
with your old, greenish rifleman's helmet.

And you will softly tell me
how as a boy
you raced paper boats
in the brown current
rushing through gutters,
how you lured the big bluebottles
with some grains of sugar
and caught them with your bare hands

and how at this moment
we are in the outskirts,
the top storey of the building
where gentle pigeons settle
along with dandelion fluff from the nearby meadows.

And then
we would climb through the hatch
out onto the roof.

Moonlight
would be stuck to the tar,
which the sun has softened during the day.

And the moon?
It would sit on the edge of the nearest chimney
and stare into the hearth's dying embers.

Holding our breaths
we will hear
how stars with their rays
pull up mushrooms in nearby forests,
how roots writhe like yellow earthworms
and how rushing streams
talk the shores into coming to the sea.

Like a bluish cotton ribbon
Zunda will lie at our feet
and in the distance
we'll see ruined factory buildings
where before the war young workers
made their living
but now lie shot dead
somewhere near Jugla or Cēsis,
or faraway Kazan, the Urals
and Crimea
and whose sons
with gentle Russians for mothers
chase geese to the Volga

through their brown village,
learn to play the guitar
and know neither their fathers
nor a word of Latvian.

Mana paradīze / *My Paradise* (1931)

For You

Lindens darken. Winds die down.
Strange weariness creeps in the weeds.
Once again you're not around
To meet me as we had agreed.

Why did you have to promise with a smile
To come at sunset to our meeting place
If you knew that all the while
You wished to visit quite another space?

You must enjoy the thought and feeling
That sick with desire I'm waiting still
While the wind sends darkness wheeling
And makes the white tracks vanish down the hill.

But maybe I should not play host
To loneliness and gloomy trends –
My good companions are the road posts,
This night and silence, silence without end.

Lindens darken. Winds die down.
Strange weariness creeps in the weeds
Once again you're not around
To meet me as we had agreed.

Mana paradīze / My Paradise (1931)

Drainpipe

Drainpipe,
you were
the first musical instrument of my boyhood,
you, five-storey-high
grey steel noodle –
a sparkling beard of ice
grows when it's cold
under your talkative mouth –
the only ice cream we boys got then for free.

You –
the winter home of all flies and centipedes,
the longest tunnel for rainwater
on its way to the slanting gutter
with its cigarette ends and apple peels.

Why do you stretch
so fragile and frail
up along house walls
like the sadness I feel?

Why are you
so thin and so gaunt
like my houseplants
and young ladies on modern postcards? –

I guess that is the fate
shared by all who strive upward
away from the hustle and bustle,
from the cheap chubby life.

Mana paradīze / My Paradise (1931)

Train

How many times
in my boyhood
I
have waited for you
by Matīss cemetery
on yellow, half-eaten hillocks,
train from St Petersburg,
train from Moscow and Tallinn
hissing like a primus,
like a water tap completely open,
covered with dust
like my clothes after a football game.

Then it seemed to me,
train,
that you
didn't run on these rails,
these two endless
silvery lines,
to reach Riga,
but instead through my soul,
my soul
and my flesh,
which trembled more
than it does now
as I caress a girl
in the shadows
behind closed curtains.

Train
when you approached,
the signalman sang
through a yellow copper horn,
holding in front of himself
a small flag
green like a chestnut leaf.

The noisy crossings,
these strange prostitutes –
free of charge
they let them –
cabbies, pedestrians, motor cars –
walk all over themselves,
upon hearing the voice of yellow copper,
they drew away quickly
from the momentary and dirty
embraces by feet and wheels
suddenly feeling love
for you alone
and
they waited for you,
alone and naked,
with barrier arms
hanging useless
by their sides –
for you –
you
train from St Petersburg
Moscow
and Tallinn –

– – – –

Train!

Mana paradīze / My Paradise (1931)

Ballad of My Joy

My anger,
Which I had been hiding in a covered bowl
Flowed into my fingertips
And I threw out
All the flowers, the phlox and the myrtle.
I drew the curtains
So that passers-by would wonder –
            is there anyone there?

I sprinkled handfuls of melancholy into the corners
And spread out yellow silk
On my greenish floor.

And here I sit, a cross-legged Turk.
Clouds, ascending overhead, crunch together.
Listen:
My joy,
What remains of it,
I put out to dry on a clothesline.
What else could I do?

So my joy hangs there with skirts and with trousers,
Along with workers' worn underwear.

A thoroughfare,
A paved highway:
My mind is a channel for my desire!

Evening.
The sun is sinking.
In the foliage, insects are quieting down,
And so does my head.
Liquid pewter gleams in windows,
The walls acquire red patches
As if in scarlet fever.
Thresholds become slippery

With the lacquer of moisture.
The chill is a knife that cuts short any breath or stench.
Darkness and the weight of stars descend on birds' wings.
The earth's breath is like heartbeat.

And then my joy
Hanging out there on the clothesline
Suddenly calls out:
– Is there anyone here
Besides the puddles and this twine?

And gentle centipedes respond,
Crawling out from their cracks into the starlight:
"Yes, there is,
Just our form isn't right,"
Then someone squeals in the rose-coloured sand:
"For the time being, there is,"
But sitting on brown, sticky fences
Tomcats meow with such misery
As if they had suffered an injury.

And then my joy goes on:
"Fine,
So look up to the right
Where lamplight pierces the opposite window.

My master has spread yellow silk
Over his greenish floor
And sits there cross-legged like a Turk
And clouds ascending over his head, crunch together.
And if someone were to put an ear to his chest,
No beating heart would be heard;
He doesn't seem to have one.

But once he was young,
He enjoyed Dutch cheese and cologne
And he felt a love so great and strong
That he could pour a lake in his hand
And raise it above the clouds;

He could collect all the scents in the world
And make violets grow on rocks.

And then he went out into the street
Where the motor car boasts of its polish.
Wearing black,
He went out
With his heart on his sleeve
And broke through the din of the street
With this speech:

'Ladies,
Listen to me,
Here's my heart,
It reaches out, it's like the sun.'

But the women
Shrugged their perfumed shoulders
And said,
Contemptuous:
'Idiot, you're an idiot,
Come to your senses,
A heart,
What will we do with a heart?
Tell us
Have you been able
To use it to buy things?
A house,
A sofa perhaps,
A rosy rug,
Or even a simple oak bed
In which we
Could lie and make love?
You can't even get
A cup of black coffee
With a heart.'

And so he stood there,
Heart in hand, on the corner.

A breeze from the sea swayed the trees.
Winds dried the sand for asphalt.
The sun covered roofs with molten silver –
That's what it did.
But he just stood there
And everyone laughed at him:
Dust, chimneys, lanterns, and pebbles,
Horse's hooves and human steps:
Boys doused him with water
But he just stood there.

Years passed.
His hands
Shrivelled and blackened.
His heart,
Silent and mute
Collapsed in on itself and melted.

And then one time,
A crow,
Bluish, keen, and hungry,
Happened to fly by.
It noticed the heart and thought it was spare.
It grabbed it
Quickly and avidly.
A lamp fell somewhere.
A wall cracked.
The day hid next to the insects amongst the leaves.

And then my master said: 'Joy,
Hey, joy,
What good are you?
If you were a spade, I could clear snow
But now?'

And so I hang here now on the clothesline
And will continue hanging
Eerie like a bat.
And all the dirt of the world will weigh on my back,

For you centipedes, animals, sand
Can't lift an axe over my head.

It's good
That it's warm for the roots under the rocks.

Iedomu spoguļi / Mirrors of Fancy (1938)

Nature

One summer,
When my heart felt strange
I left for the countryside.

All day long,
I wandered through forests and fields,
I drank from creeks
Ate berries,
And my feet turned into oak bark.

And one time
When, lying in the grass,
I watched winds weave a cloud,
I met a man,
An old man
With a spade over his shoulder.

Hearing about my strange heart,
He said:
'Come with me, son,
Let's do some work.'
And his words made dandelions
Scatter their fluff.

And so
All summer
I worked deep in the forest,
Digging beds for streams.

And now?

Now
I stand in the middle of a boulevard
With a smile:
I have no worries.

A tart can address me
Or a wandering Jew,
A passer-by, an urchin, a gentleman can push me,
A tram or a motorcar can splash me –
It doesn't matter.

All summer I lay in moss,
I caressed roots,
Told stories to mushrooms,
And cleared dew from leaves.

All summer, the moon wove gold in my eyes
And eternity
Lay like a leaf on my forehead.

Even now,
My fingers smell of honey,
Calm lies in my heart
Like seeds in an apple
And my mind shelters
Lake's sparkling mists and
The scents of high noon.

Iedomu spoguļi / Mirrors of Fancy (1938)

Where I Will Sit Tonight

My darling,
Tonight I will sit at your feet
On a yellow pillow.

We will rob the lamp of its bulb
To feel only the moon's caress.

Look,
The sky is as blue
As the stained glass in rich stairwells.
And stars?
Are they not the flashlights
Of all the city boys
Searching for a lost puppy?

You know,
Cafés are now full of blue smoke
As if they were floating through clouds.
We will sit there alone –
But you want to hear music?
Listen to the tram hum on the street,
To water drip from the pump.

Your knees are warm as breath.
Your hands on my cheeks
Are fragrant dreams.

And your parted lips
Entice
The air of the room
That smells of myrtle
And landlady's furniture.

My darling,
Tonight I will sit at your feet
On a yellow pillow.

I Yearn for Another Form

More and more,
I don't want to be human.
Exhausting.
I would like to become
A rose-coloured flamingo
In faraway Cairo.

Or I could be a small house
For just three families,
Or a chair leg
Bound to break soon.

More and more,
I don't like to be human.
All the various passions
Are disappearing for me.

I wish I were a corner
Covered in spiderwebs.
Or simple dough,
Or an orange cactus.

Or I could be a flat cake
Or the floor of my room:
Then I wouldn't even get up
In the morning.

Sun would go down inside me.
A dog would sniff at me.
I would tear at the soles.
But there is no way,
In vain do I torture my brain.

I'm only a human,
Insignificant, small.
And what is my strength?
It's nothing at all.

A grasshopper hops
Ten times its size.
In vain, I ask for a star to land on my hand:
I can only burn on my own.

If I could prick the sunset sky,
To have their wine flow into me.
Then I would raise my heart as a flower
To be broken by the wind.

So that its fragile fragrance would
Fill the space,
Telling them all how fierce was the heart
That was mine.

Iedomu spoguļi / Mirrors of Fancy (1938)

The Ring

And then you entered
Sashaying like a streetwalker
Whose womb beckons like death.

You entered.

Linden leaves gleamed with world's breath.
Somewhere underground,
In basements,
Mice scurried squeaking
And sawdust in their fur
Sparkled like gold.

You entered and said to me:
        – I will come tonight. –
And birds pulsed through the sky like warm blood.
Over the city, buildings, and steamers,
I
Breathed in the sea,
And sweat from the edges of clouds
Settled between my lips,
And sand blown over my lips by the wind
I crunched between my teeth.

        – I will come tonight –
These words
Went straight to my heart,
And made me tremble like dew.

Evening.

I covered the windows.
All the windows.

Trying to protect my heart,
I hid it on a shelf

Among books greying with age,
Among memories and empty glasses.
All at once I lit
Three long candles –
Red, blue, and black.
I covered the bed with a yellow, porous
Blanket, which soaks up
Sweat, moans, and desire;
And next to the bed,
I placed a bench
Where your flowing robes could be thrown
And hidden under a copper vase.

And then you entered
Fierce and swift like a draught,
Like a heavy and lingering scent.

You entered.

From your passion,
The blanket lying on the floor naked
Curled up like birch bark.
Flames pulled away from the candles
And fled into the dark.

You entered.
And with a quiet smile,
You picked up
My heart from the shelf,
Blew on it
And then put it on your finger like a ring.

A ring on your finger.

Iedomu spoguļi / Mirrors of Fancy (1938)

Mirror of Fancy

Firewood gets cheaper by the day.
What does it matter
Where I sit with my soda-water?
Vainly,
Vainly you try to scare me with death.

It doesn't matter that I wander in tatters
And the sky is so pale overhead;
It doesn't matter that for three hours straight
I have to fish for my very last coin
And, hand outstretched like a plate,
I feed my brain to the Andean eagles.

Higher,
And higher still
With my fantasy skis
Above that which you love so much:
Above money and clothes,
Above where people kiss.

Eternity,
You,
You intoxicate me more
Than lovage in my boyhood.

You,
Eternity,
I send you my eyes.

I feel
I'm shrinking and losing my size.
Even now I can try
To become an earthworm in the soil.
Even now,
I hold ten mountains in my hand
And support the universe with my toil.

Bring me all the snows of Greenland,
So that I can turn them to water
With the breath from my lungs!
Or do you want me to light your candles
With a stalk of wheat?

Dreams,
They are love,
Love
That brought me these verses with grace.
From behind the slanting woodpile,
The sun leaps down like yellow tomcat
To lick at my face.

I feel so good on the ground I roll,
And above my head
A telegraph pole
Plays its harmonica.

Iedomu spoguļi / *Mirrors of Fancy* (1938)

My Roach Ensemble

My dear,
For you, I'd become a donkey in Tibet.
And you?
You just grin and file at your fingernails.
My soul is a speck of dust on your hem.

It's bad:
Just now,
My mind is ill and sad.
Shall I start up a bierkeller
And, if it fails,
Something even less stellar?
It's bad.
To try to please you,
I tried this approach:
I bought a dozen roaches
And set them loose in my room.
Now they walk around all brown
On floor and walls without a frown.
Then
I used spittle to polish an old mirror
To make the reflections clearer.
Then I put honey on top
And they could perform without stopping.

When you feel restless,
Come,
My dear,
Come to me.
Everything,
But everything is the same.
For your shoulders, my dame,
There will be the velvet shawl
To protect you against draught's crawl,
I keep my rose tea in there;
You will sit in my grandpa's red chair

And you will note
In the blue dusk of my room
My roaches' soft coo,
Quieter than sugar dove's.
And outside, my love,
My single hen will gaze in with greed.
When my room gets too dark,
You think I'll despair?
I will not care!
A thin slice of white bread
Will be our lamp overhead.
All things will take on a strange form –
And myself?
An old key from the gate
I will play like the flute.
Sounds will pour out in sharp little drops.
And then,
My dear,
In the glow of the room,
In the looking-glass,
My trained roaches in mass
Will begin –
Noble and proud as peacocks –
Liszt's *Hungarian Dances* and Grieg's *Åse's Death*.

World, hold your breath!

And if you,
My dear,
Would only laugh about it a little,
You know,
My heart would no longer feel so brittle.
And I would take my pupils
And leave without any scruples.
In the dives of Hamburg,
Where the damp air pricks one's lungs
Like a cactus,
My roaches would practise:
They would dance a waltz,

Leap over a burning logs with no faults,
They would fly
And sing English songs at high pitch.

Sailors
In their glee
Would snatch pipes
From each other's teeth;
But as for me,
I would collect money
For you, honey,
In a big copper bowl.
But then,
(Oh, I'd rather recite a sentimental song!)
My competitor will do me a wrong:
He will buy my best waiter.
And on a sunny morning
As my roaches are still sleeping
In their Japanese silk bed,
A green, deathly powder he'll spread.
And even if I'd rub them with the best spirits,
It would be without merit:
They would die in agony
And by their box of ebony
I will stand
Together with two Finnish trainers,
With armfuls of fine flowers.
We will buy them
In the Hamburg insect graveyard.
It will be April in the air
And trees budding over there.
And what about me?
Do you think
I would be
Fishing for roaches?
No!
I will be hungry
And out of money.
God, why did you give me a soul?

And then,
My dear,
To forget about you –
My greatest love and misery –
I would drag myself to the port.
There I would become a rope,
A strong, oily rope,
Waiting for an axe
That will use its might
To cut me in two one night.

The end.

Morning.
A huge fountain pen drawing night's black ink from the sky.

Iedomu spoguļi / Mirrors of Fancy (1938)

Restlessness

Trees bud,
In green arcs they rise toward the sun.
Can I bud with them?

My toes as roots I would put down into the soil –
Right here, on the boulevard, in the street!
And live
With windows the brightness of wind.

I drink, I breathe, I want, and I move.
I see crosses on Latgalian roads,
Birds that fly over African fields
Covered in dust,
Seas that uncover their rose-coloured rocks
In their depths.
But I know no peace.

And at night,
At the hour
When deer find their watering site,
When eternity drips onto every worm,
I feel
I stand
        in the middle of a
                great, dark square
Where I played ball as a child
And where it smelled of horses, wild.

Stars push off from my head,
Pigeons seek warmth under my chin,
The sky is the blue
            of a human vein,
Yet there is no joy in my soul.
I hear graves cave in,
Water quietening in gutters.
Humidity settles on pebbles like silver.

My skin crawls with chill.
But I know no peace.

And then I go
Green with exhaustion
I go
To dark alleyways
Where bitter revelry is sold,
Where problems are solved
With a switchblade,
But I know no peace.

And then, with my tie jutting –
It safeguards my pride –
I go to a coffeehouse.
From the radio it's clear: cherries bloom in Yokohama,
Pink fish swim in the rivers,
But I sit,
Just sit,
Drinking prickly soda-water for two,
And I know no peace.

The bluish aroma of coffee
Stares like eternity, heavy and crazy,
It stares
Making my mind all hazy,
Pouring the dark over my fingernails
And crumpling my dreams like paper.

And then suddenly
I feel like crumbling all glasses in my hand,
Insulting a guest
Pouring the contents over his head,
But I sit here like a pewter cast,
I sit here
Without knowing why my tie keeps jutting out.

It's freezing.
The music keeps unrolling a sad tango,

In crystal vases
          flowers keep fading.
And I have no peace.
I feel
How women's vulvas ripen under their clothes,
Drunkards hide their hearts in their glasses.
In a street in Chicago,
Tardy walkers vanish home
And deserts tremble and cough
From the stings of sun rays.

And then I see –
All clock hands grow like masts
And cut into my heart.

And then I see –
Like a terrible tail
My tongue
Rises and beats
Against all global shores
With an abrupt little shout:
'Where's the sun?'
I shake
And I dissolve in the last drop of my shout.

'Aren't you a funny one – the sun…
See? It floats like a slice of lemon
In your very glass,'
Says a waitress coming over.
Lacquer carnation blooms on her fingers and breath –
Just lacquer.

The stench of dust and blood
Swells over the world.
My pulse stops.
Stars darken and turn to soil.
People take aim.
There's no peace.
I'm freezing.

In vases all over the world
        flowers are fading.

Iedomu spoguļi / *Mirrors of Fancy* (1938)

Letter to a Dead Newspaper Woman
Address: Ziepniekkalns Cemetery

My letter will not be very long
And I will write it in big letters.
I wonder,
Do you have a pair of glasses up there?
People are strange,
They cry at funerals
And fail to see
What a dead person might need.

Forgive me
That I don't know where your grave is.
When you died I was away
And when, upon returning to Iļģuciems,
I went to your house
No one knew anything about you.
Your granddaughter had gone to the countryside
To work.
She has a baby now,
You know –
From that no-good Black Janka (grandma sighs as she reads this).

He doesn't show any concern,
Just keeps smoking
Chewing sunflower seeds
And playing the mandolin.
The baby is very weak.
It would be best if you took it in.

I haven't forgotten you.
Always,
When I walk past that corner
Where you squatted low and wide like a bush,
I recall your face
Covered with tiny wrinkles,
Your quaking, singing voice

And your thank-yous
Crawling with the divine as if with ants.

I know what you would like to ask me.
Since you died,
The Iļģuciems house where you lived
Is still much the same.
The landlord
Simply gave a new coat of paint to the outside,
And old Mrs Ilsters
Went to live with the Kanenieks clan.

On the corner
Where you used to sit,
There is now a small brown kiosk,
Almost childlike.
A girl sits inside,
Young, with blond, shiny hair.
She knows how to smile
And, as she hands out the news,
She shows her sleek, delicate fingers
With a fine, sunny skin.

The kiosk business is going well.
But the young men
Who come to shop there,
Linger too long.
And, as they walk away,
Their faces are aglow, all strangely lit up.

My poet friends,
When they got the news of your death,
Got drunk in a bar,
Broke glasses,
Talked rubbish
And called you the newspaper mama.
Don't get upset.
What else could they do?
Go to the church,

Put a wreath on the spot where you sat,
Get all sad?
They are weak.

Your prescription for rheumatism – kerosene oil –
Doesn't work for me.
My right knee keeps making sounds
As if someone inside there
Were doing his nails.
But let's talk about that
When I'm up there with you.

And that may be soon.
A new world war is afoot.
I will go to the front
And then maybe to you.
But it doesn't matter,
Long enough I've quarrelled,
And kissed girls,
Long enough I've been fearful, unwanted,
It's enough,
I would have nothing against
Going up there to be with you.

There we would play cards,
Eat bonbons that you are so fond of.
And when we'd tire of that,
I would sing to you of Transvaal
And play the guitar.

In the evening,
I would bring you water
For your old myrtles and phlox.
Let me know
If you haven't broken a pot or two;
When I come, I could bring you
A new one for you.
Now I'll close.

If you can't
Read my letter after all,
Get Jānis Ziemeļnieks –
He'll help you.
He's a slender, nice young man
With dark glasses
And he answers to – Poet.

Iedomu spoguļi / *Mirrors of Fancy* (1938)

Soul Fisher

I hear: someone is walking
Singing about the Daugava rapids,
About the current in the river so avid.

The sounds flow blunt and fast,
The air envelops my skin
Like a sack filled with sharp pins,
Stabbing my breath, my mind and my eyes.

The song's honey-sweet pie
Has turned all bitter and pale.
What made it so pungent and stale?
Is it the horror dried up in the mud?
Or is it the foreboding of blood?

The lonely walker is singing a song
About what happened – it hasn't been long:
How the Germans crossed the big river.

Why stick a bayonet into my heart?
Where is the sweet of your tongue?
Why do you cut off my breath?

Put away the time that is past
Like a rose that wilts and won't last.

Yet the sad, lonesome walker
Doesn't begin a new song.

He just keeps walking along
With a face that could not be older,
And with a net over his shoulder
That seems to be slightly aslant.

He goes on with his harsh chant:
– O river, bed to slain souls. –

The ground boils under his soles.

Perhaps it is just a grim story,
Yet indeed there is something gory:
He puts the heavy nets into the stream,
Where schools of fish swift as dreams
Run to the sea! to the sea!

He goes on with his harsh chant:
– O river, bed to slain souls. –

The brown dough down the riverbanks
Runs to the sea! to the sea!

The Kausupe, Ķekava, Iecava,
The beauties of forest and heath,
Hold their waves and don't dare breathe,
Seeing the fisher wade with his seine
Into the Daugava after the slain.

Should someone ask of this man:
– What do you do with this net?
He is ready to tell
With a voice gruff, out of hell:
– My nets are picking up souls
In battle that fell
One by one. –

His nets tremble along with the sky.
A wave rolls to the shore, surly and high.

Without any fear of cold and of death,
Singing his song, he goes on his way
Where the Island of Death
Lies enshrouded, foggy and grey.

He goes on with his harsh chant:

– O river, bed to slain souls,
When will you yield to my nets
The many hearts of the Letts
By the Island of Death?

From the Daugava depths,
From that bluest of seams,
I will lift heroes' breaths
With my finest of nets. –

He goes on chanting in vain,
Moving around his seine.
The waters – they are too deep,
And lost are those in there, asleep.

The Kausupe, Ķekava, Iecava,
The beauties of forest and heath,
Hold their run and don't dare breathe
Seeing the fisher wade with his seine
Into the Daugava after the slain.

The rivers see the time draw near
When the fisher's brow will be clear
And when he will lift from the depths
All the slain souls' breaths
And hold them up to the sky.
Eternity will descend from up high
And turn to poetry all these lives.

from *Mūžības skartie / Touched by Eternity* (1940)

Night Visitor

The night visitor is the first fallen rifleman, Jēkabs Voldemārs Timma of Biķernieki. Timma enlisted as a volunteer in the 2nd Company of the First Daugavgrīva Latvian Riflemen's Battalion. He fell in battle on October 15, 1915 by the Kraslovski homestead.

September. A chilly night. Biķernieki.
The blue is strewn with golden pebbles.
The glow of Riga, a gigantic rose petal,
Breathing in the distance. Midnight.
Biķernieku Street is empty,
Only on the corner, at its source,
Where gorgeous lindens ascend the blue,
Something flickers above the pavement,
Next to fences, over blooms and empty furrows,
Something airy, vibrating like steam,
It touches panes and entrance thresholds;
It forms an outline and keeps perusing
The moist pavement, shining underneath.
The pebbles think he must be trying
To open up some thought as if a door.

Then suddenly it lurches forward
Past the houses lining Biķernieku Street,
Which points like a finger toward timelessness.
Wherever he moves, he leaves a trace in space;
The trace that blooms, then slowly melts away.

Is it a ghost or is it a giant beast
That breathes down this smallish street?
Is it vapours from the brow of God?
Who knows. The condensed light
Glides fast and the tranquil moonlight
Shines on his strange trajectory –
Over objects, reason, space.
All along the street sand and houses wonder.
Silence follows, embracing him
Then seeping through him like a shiny wave.

And when he stands there, at the top of Biķernieku,
All alone, midnight on his shoulder,
He is lashed by something gentle.
Tenderness greets and embraces him warmly,
Making him tremble, freeze and then vibrate again.

He begins to sense and feel all things,
All the scents, the swath of fog.
What matter the past, time and dust?
A light breeze, a smile on one's lip – and that's it.

He feels: nothing is gone for him,
Not the land, his native land,
Fences, trees, houses, and thresholds,
People and birds, the beautiful distance,
All that which made him live and laugh,
All that which was touched by his breath –
All is gathering around him now;
In a fiery stream and fervent haste,
It all is rising in his heart and lifting him
Up in fluff and stars, and sky, and joy.

The uncommon strength that flows into him
Splits him into the atoms of the soil.
He now feels himself in every pebble,
In every stone, in every fragrant needle,
In every waft of air that settles on his lips.

All depths are signalling welcome,
Lakes lift up their wombs,
Trees twine their roots around his heart,
Yielding sap that turns into a thirst,
Into blood and arduous intent.

He is aware now: his ghost is vanishing,
He's turning into a human, like he was before.
He feels: he's ripening like a grain well into soil.
His flesh senses, it's becoming flesh
Clad into old and greying warrior's clothes,
Full of quickened blood and hot desires.

He feels his breath embraced anew
By distances and fading grit of midnight,
Homeland's silences, so crisp and peaceful,
The smell of pavement, manure's poignant stench,
The pebbly pavement, side-street dwellings.

It all flows into him in an endless stream,
And he succumbs himself
In a brown and steaming whiff.

O, the change! Time can never crack it,
The sword can never cut it. Or death conceal it.

And with every step he takes, he is more and more
A man, flesh, blood, and desire.
Where like a shadow or a candle flame
He first fluttered among objects
Like steam he was transparent and like living breath,
Now he takes firm and clear-cut strides,
His body slim, flesh dry and warmly clad,
And hurried in his gestures and his breath.

In the palm of space his body gleams
As if made of silver and thrown
On this earth to stand against.

Gray pallor settles on his youthful face.
Hair's turned gray on his brow and temple.
Strange and fiery gleam his eyes
Reflecting scenes and images
Arriving, flashing, leaving in a hurry.

And he sees – where once there were fields,
Where as a boy he ran around and fought,
There now stand houses with misty, shiny panes.

But to his right, he senses with his body,
On Little Biķernieku, further down,
Timma house stands, built by his father,

Across the meadow, amongst some trees,
As always by the roadside,
With a sun-burnt flesh,
And small, tear-streaked windows,
With grass and lovage sprouting at the corners. He feels
It was not in vain, his lengthy walk here
From the graveyard, from the nether world, and over
Along the railway, over Čiekurkalns,
Over the streets and trees, and the light.

He feels he could die again with no less passion
Than he, the first to fall, had done that other time.

How can these humdrum yards,
The empty plain, potato rows,
Damp cobblestones, smoke hanging in the trees
Embrace him, lift him up to where
There is no sense of life or even death?

The old mud falls off his feet, retreating,
His clothing is like new, full of lustre,
With his great coat soft like downy willow catkin.

He is already past Stirnas street that's new,
Past the houses vaguely fuming,
Past youngish trees and the cruelty of fences.

And then he's at the gate of Timma's household,
Which last he touched so long ago;
His hand feels warm and tingling,
The wound is burning like a star.
Sloughed off, the old pain falls
Into grass. Opening, the gate squeaks softly.
The ground steams underfoot. The well is
An eager mouth bestowing kisses,
The barn is painting on a smile.

He walks on slowly, leans into the pane.
Looms above the window, the same old ash.

With its leaves, it's chasing off his neck
The feeble, bluish light shed by the moon.

Inside, he hears a baby softly crying.
A door squeaks, a young woman enters.
He's never seen her, she must be his brother's wife.

A white, protective wing, she leans ov'r the child;
Strange mist seeps in his eyes. The wind
Must have splashed his cheek with dew,
Sweet, velvety and gentle like a bee.

A minute more and then another window.
He stares long through its brownish pane,
His eyes taking in each and every thing,
Breathing in to his very heart each whiff of air
That the panes are feebly letting out.

That's how he circles round the house,
And walking by, his undamaged hand caresses
Each stem of grass, each mote of dust.

His fingers press the paint closer to the wood,
His palm stamps kisses on the house's walls,
He inhales its old smell deeply,
Eyes storing deep its looming bulk;
Then he steps back to take it all away
With his very breath and to the end.

He turns away and walks around the yard,
Treading long across its brow,
As if to fully cover with his trace
This pale and frosted-over space;
As if to pick up with his glance
Each wood chip, puddle, tiny straw
That shimmers in the moonlight.

He then walks to the barn and stays a while
In its warm and scented dark.

He tells something to the weary fowl,
Says something to the cow and whispers to the horse.
And then he vanishes inside the shed
That's full of hay, old saddles
And buckets, carts, and heavy yokes.
He wants to hold in, view it all,
To feel it, embrace it with his every tissue
And to bring it, like a kiss, back underground.

Each and every thing he touches,
Smiles back at him like at a treasured guest,
Blooming like a flower at its prime,
As if a reddish glow were washing over it,
As if the sky and warmth were beckoning.

And when finally he stops at the middle,
Having seen it all with his own eyes,
A smile settles on his lips like a star.
His chest is breathing easy,
Hands turning pink, caressed by things,
His clothes suffused with fresh and lovely scents.

He stands there large and heavy like the earth.
His feet, two axes buried in the soil.
He throws his head back over all of Riga,
Nape propped against the Biķernieki woods.
In the depths of Linezers his hand is plunged,
Same lake, the fount of strength for him in boyhood,
His clothing parts to meet the autumn winds,
He could embrace them and the entire space.

So there he stands with penetrating eyes,
Looking deep into what his death has wrought:
The hot, steaming soil of native Latvia.
But, to take it all in before departing
In one fresh and sprightly sip,
He lifts his head off the forests,
Opening his chest, stretching out his arms,
Drawing breath down to his heart.

And then it comes from all corners of the land:
From flat Zemgale and distant river Venta,
From blue Rauna pines, Gaiziņš hill and Rāzna lake,
From all the borderlands and shores:
The air and people's breath,
Cattle smells, aromas of all things,
Water vapours and the poignant stench of soil,
Enveloping him and blending in a single breath.

But as he tries to take this penetrating breath
And store it in his heart like a treasured bloom,
He notices there something alien and rude –
There is harsh bitterness inside it
And it fires up his blood and mind.
He feels it from his fingertips to toes:
The harsh bitterness is hostile to this land.
It is the same enemy that killed him once
And made him lie in that grave for many years.

He feels the bite of lead that cut his heart,
The wound burning in his hand.
And he knows full well what's to be done.

When he hears the growling
Of the old dog by his feet,
He holds the dog's head gently
Like a bowl most exquisite.
He takes him to the shed where by the doghouse
The chain gleams cold and idle in the straw.
Turning over the dog to its weighty power,
He says: – From now on, I will guard the house. –

Decisive, he then walks up to the door,
Wakes his brother, sister, children
And lights a candle on the table.
He takes off his hat and smooths his hair;
Its silver sparkles like a white hot flame.

His people gather round him, pale,
The words that come slide off the tongue,
Falling back in breath like something jagged.
Shake his hand? Push over a chair?
Make the children kiss his hand?

The candle flame turns the window
And all the objects into shadows
Looming on the floor, in corners, over thresholds.

Finally, he says in a gravelly voice:

— Don't be afraid, I am still your brother,
I have come here for just an instant,
To see how you are faring here, in the Timma household,
To touch all the things I've loved
And can't forget even as I lie there dead.
Keep safe, my people, my passion is still with you
And my blood is still living in this house.

Don't forget my death and hold it fast:
I feel a morbid stench in air.
And when the danger comes to our house,
Remember me, for I will always be
A burning light above the gate of Timma's,
Guarding you and our native land,
And nothing then will overpower you.

Having said this, he is gone. Just the candle flame
Begins to flicker: both doors
open wide to the anteroom and yard.
Winds freely enter now on flapping wings
And chase away the dusty smell.

But right above the street, just like before,
A strange light flickers, creeping home.

from *Mūžības skartie* / *Touched by Eternity* (1940)

Speck of Dust

I became a speck of dust and very light in weight.
I settled on a goat's distinguished horn.
It was a pleasant seat. And it made me laugh:
There was this sweet and tranquil goaty smell.

I saw it all – there was nothing closed for me:
Grieving souls, the fading warmth.
A thrush that landed in a sheltered tree
Then yelled at me: 'Be quiet, earthly trifle!'

Smiling I replied: 'Shut your hungry beak
Like the worn covers of a dusty book!
Yes, I'm a speck of dust. The beginning and the end.
Like a grain of wheat I gleam: I am the germ of all!'

The thrush then went quiet and rushed away.
If I'm a speck of dust, then all is possible for me.
I can change my form and grab him like a hand.
A red, dangling apple will be his death knell.

Zem cēlās zvaigznes / Under the Noble Star (1948)

Lightning Source UK Ltd.
Milton Keynes UK
UKHW010748291221
396330UK00001B/100